STANDOFF

STANDOFF   *Poems*

David Rivard

Graywolf Press

This publication is made possible, in part, by the voters of Minnesota through a Minnesota State Arts Board Operating Support grant, thanks to a legislative appropriation from the arts and cultural heritage fund, and through a grant from the Wells Fargo Foundation Minnesota. Significant support has also been provided by Target, the McKnight Foundation, the Amazon Literary Partnership, and other generous contributions from foundations, corporations, and individuals. To these organizations and individuals we offer our heartfelt thanks.

Published by Graywolf Press
250 Third Avenue North, Suite 600
Minneapolis, Minnesota 55401

www.graywolfpress.org

Published in the United States of America

ISBN 978-1-55597-745-0

2 4 6 8 9 7 5 3 1
First Graywolf Printing, 2016

Library of Congress Control Number: 2015953718

Cover design: Michaela Sullivan

Cover art: Philip Guston (1913–1980). *Source.* 1976. Oil on canvas, 75" x 117". Gift of Edward R. Broida in honor of Uncle Sidney Feldman. The Museum of Modern Art. Copyright © The Estate of Philip Guston. Digital image © The Museum of Modern Art. Licensed by SCALA / Art Resource.

in memory of my father,
Norman Rivard

&

Steve Orlen
Stephen Berg
Tomaž Šalamun

CONTENTS

                          It
moved me, that
life was after all
like that. You are

in love. You stand
in the woods, with
a horse, bleeding.
The story is true.

—Robert Creeley

STANDOFF

GREENWOOD NIGHTFALL

I miss myself most
these days with friends
I feel a distance from
when talking to;
but for the moment
I get to stand here
clear-eyed & cold
inside the murderous
machinery of our birthright—
I get to breathe the thin air
all have had to breathe
these past two hundred years,
not the oxygen
we dreamed of, that
hothouse air. In the telenovella
based on my life
tall prairie grasses bent
by an Alberta wind
would sprawl snugly
I've been told
behind a woman vaulting
in blue pajama bottoms.
Does any of this have
anything to do with me
at all? Nightfall,
nightfall without giggles
or binary code—
greenwood nightfall—
that's what calls me now?

LESS THAN, MORE THAN

Where am I going today
if I'm going anywhere at all
without my soul,
that bird with its unreadable, unheard name
having wandered off again,
convinced that it is more than just a word—
do we travel far from each other today?—
me in my pre-owned Mazda
with my radio full of wasps' nest news,
my Peshawar & my Rupert Murdoch,
all my guilty Murdochs—
my destination
like a homestead made of
fallen maple leaves,
the three leaves that form a tipi
tipped together
by a 5-year-old's hands,
a dwelling place,
where if I wanted to
I could rest my human rights
while my soul
travels far from its base, lost for a while
on its own highly privatized trip,
the idea of living forever
an idea that is not an eternity at all
for my wanderer
but a wish the bird has
to fly brocaded by herself
within the borders of a tapestry,
far from some witch queen's cackle,

far from that witch
who has disguised herself as a sparhawk
woven out of dark thread
by a Flemish peasant's hands—
      how far is too far, you ask?—
a little foolishness
goes a long, long way, I'd say;
a lot drops dead
in its tracks.

SAID

I fed my father what
as it turned out the future
would call his last meal
(tho at the time neither
he nor I was required to
think of it that way exactly)—
ground chourico & chopped
green pepper open-faced
on a burger bun, french fries,
a cupcake with icing almost
chocolate in flavor—alarming,
a departure from his diet
of low-sodium, zeroed-out
trans fats & sugar-free
vegetables with high fiber-
scores, suffering as he had
been for years from barbarian
cholesterol & geriatric
diabetes (the nurse shrugged
simply & said "why not?"—
meaning of course that
we should get it, all of us,
he *was* going to die,
and soon). A few loose
chitters of ground sausage
fell onto his johnnie
from the fork I lifted
to his mouth—they left
tiny, paprika-red dots
of oil on the sheer cotton,

prussic red, corpuscle red
like the small scabs my sister
and I had left on his face
while helping him shave
the day before. A week earlier
I had visited him at home;
the day an unusually warm
day in a March unusually
cold. He was telling me how
he'd gone out into the yard
to get some sun only to return
minutes later to the house,
the wind far too strong—
he said he'd worried that
if the wind took his hat
from his head, he might
die while chasing it.
I made a joke—forced to,
I thought—chasing a hat,
I said, that might be
a better death than most,
I said maybe the death
certificate would read "killed
by the wind." He laughed
all right. You know, he said,
you've really got a lousy
sense of humor. Better than
nothing, I guess—(did *he*
say *that*, or did I think
it?). Later he said . . . he'd said

earlier ... then I said ... he
said ... I said ... I said ...
I said. ... Say now that
this might be all that's left
for consolation, this
might be love at the end,
the confidences exchanged—
all these pratfalls, & this
skin chapped by a blade,
and your willing servant's
shaky hands, then a short
trip to be washed a last,
finally blameless time
(so the scriptures say)
in the blood of the lamb:
a smell like the smell of
sweetgrass burning crosswise
the length of a dry plain
and sent by a wind whose
swiftness has in it the bright
voices of kindergarteners, children
born of a hardship town.

BIRTH CHART

to Simone

Wandering off under those astrological signs
charted just for you, my quiet trekker—all
those houses & planets so perfectly straight-faced
but still baffling at birth—don't think badly
of me when I'm dead & you've gone deep
into the distance of love tangles, moneyed
interests, & old-fashioned commutes—into life
in other words—I did what I could for you, knowing
it might not be enough—I see now that I can't
save you from suffering, & that trying to hurts
if I'm not kind. Tho I still want your life to be
untroubled, & am afraid for you, a fear made
out of my own fear of a future I can't control—
the world so often a human heart that eats itself—
places like New Orleans the Swat Valley Fukushima—
the names of those remote destinations for film crews
and symposium panels are places people die
native to those regions & out to kill or defend
life from itself—there is so much misery there
that refuses to call itself misery & that sees itself
instead as the unimpeachable power of a righteous day.
And there are criminals & dunces elsewhere—
hideous partyline whips, Saxon in outlook
and proud of it—there are the bodysnatched
and the inane candy-stripers & the greedy
and the martini narcissists high on the rising year—
but let's take the long view: these are not
your true companions, & out of my reach your
life will make itself in struggle & love perhaps

dependent on the strength that will come
if I only let go when you step out the door
as hazel-eyed now as always & maybe more so
this morning in slate-gray Gore-Tex.

SWERVER

She was born for
the pleasures of swerving
and with a courage
as impractical as it was
necessary
beneath a harsh lightbulb
in some Alberta hotel,
not to play the fool
or push a hangman's cart.
She remembers
how summers there
had the excitable, slipshod languor
of strip poker,
but that winter snapped
like a brown rat trapped & frantic
in a wooden cage, a cage
she'd last seen flying through dark smoke,
her father having flipped it
with one furious hand onto a bonfire.
So it goes with
the impossible—
at 16 you think yourself
a connoisseur
of the inner-life for sure,
tho you're allowed
an occasional glimpse of the world
and how it looks
to others—10,000 colors
in the skin of an apple,
and not one of them red or green—

name one
and the future might
open for a moment in spite of all
your evil speculations.
She remembers her mother
drowned the ticks in a mason jar
after they'd been pulled
from the garrison dogs,
the jar half-full of machine oil.
The first boy she kissed
spoke of superhumans & died later
of a brain hemorrhage.
She remembers all of this later.
Later—
after much statecraft had taken place,
and days that passed
like the sound of swan's wings in the fog
whenever she sat
by herself at a foreign picnic table.

RYE WHISKEY, RYE WHISKEY

A switchyard walk at twilight—

waiting for the freight cars
to rattle past & the wheels to melt a penny

I've placed on the rail—an experiment in transformation

widely available to homeschoolers—

study of the thousand & more hurts that need
to be endured, an unspooling infinity of such, in support
of so many changes.

You can't explain transience
to a child otherwise,

or the purpose of our momentums—

i.e., friction:
even in water

a rubbing away occurs
during the wanderings of a jellyfish,

swirling & round, tendrilled

for filtering, & highly capable
in currents swept along long miles

of Norse beachhead—
on every beach

the iodine tang of red seaweed,
and cormorants

spreading their wings to dry, putting the squeeze on,

pompous, but getting lighter & more nubile.

Once you've learnt in childhood
that the world is built

out of shiftings & abrasions
you see how
you'll have to make allowances—

so I can't forget
the smell of my grandfather's freshly perked
Maxwell House just after

he'd poured a jigger of rye
into his mug,

and how it kindled the morning air,

pleasantly,

but with consequences.

PLAY SAFE

Thinking of
Dean in Austin,
new heart in his chest—
old heart beached on some larkspurred Viking coastline—
in seclusion
2-3 months so
his immune system can get
corrected & reset—
if I write him maybe
I should put the sheets of paper & envelope
in an oven prior to mailing the letter,
all the pathogens & microbes
stunned, baked sterile at something just below
Fahrenheit 451—
what else, rub sheets readable with Purell?—
"play safe" says
the graffiti tagged
on the mailbox
nearest my house, under
a magic-markered & defanged mouse drawn
with translucent condom pulled
over his head all the way down to ankles,
wide punchline smile
on his face,
put there by the minx-
cast spell of some no-nonsense
jeune fille—
Dean is no mouse tho:
dear retrofit friend
on a street

where 2 mismatched shoes got left
at the entrance
of some dark quayside alley,
right-sized
just so a live man twice
as alive
with a dead man's
heart
can walk on now.

TAKE IT ON THE HEEL

Whatever else might make itself
available, some nightlife
takes place solely within the nutshell
space of the mind—
March 6th, it's a beer garden
for worriers
desperate for peace,
where street sweeper & bounty hunter alike
take a hike for company
and brewed bat's piss—
the Manchurians know nothing of Munich,
neither do Manicheans,
but plenty of them know waking at 3 a.m.
with unleashed thoughts,
a pack of hounds on your heels
until you tire out the dogs,
fall back asleep—
what's it all for?
Honestly, do I really think it makes
me a better person
to lie there dope-slapped by past mistakes
or anxious for getting
right with some future I imagine
looming?—
no, I gave up on that long ago—
it's the quarrelsome
blind man inside
my feelings,
gone out for a stroll, obsessively needy,
taking it on the heel.

DON'T

Don't doubt it when the core samples prove
how pleasing it would be to be woken by a baster's
rain at dawn, cool grass wet with the benign.
Your tormentors are yet to be born, or fell asleep
a millennium ago. Your beauty is the beauty
that does not dispense with struggles—it wears
loafers the color of gun-metal, a face full of
second thoughts, eyes you'd like to believe
are supernatural. Agreed: aspiring to eyes of a color
not found in nature *is* very lace-curtain Irish,
and you *do* resemble one of Yeats's twilight boys,
the walk cold from counting house to pub,
the Easter Rising over—but the purpose of your days
isn't simply to meet cute, it's to be changed.
We inherit a marshalling yard full of dark freight,
but the track switches work. How much of whomever
you are after all is who you were when you
were the stony theologian of Westport Harbor?
Maybe in a quiet moment in the backyard today
you'll look at a spray of tea roses leafing out
and hear the rain inside them whenever a breeze
blows. Don't let possibility go away in pain.

STOWAWAYS

Tho it's true our fathers' fathers nailed to their doors
wreaths of pagan balsam on plowed city streets
far from dark pines they were not winsome—
and as the offspring of their momentum
neither are we—do we look like pretty boys
or missionaries to you?—no church bells will
ever ring us home, our months held hostage
by some warlord over—and we aren't about to
hatch a plan to rid the town of bribery either—
there are no martyrs here among us; a single flash
of lightning would show you that—so if
you're looking to us now for reparations, you'd best
look somewhere else—we don't believe in cheating,
but we often cook the books—we have
the ready gifts we all were born with, for better
or worse—even if each of us has woken at night
and felt himself an immigrant still, with little
to call his own but a stowaway's code,
a cold window to touch his forehead to & cry.
We can tell ourselves that at least we knew
the difference between sleeping & waking—
but the snow can see that from a distance
we look like all the distance it's fallen through.

IRON RISING OUT OF IRON

Everywhere in Boston by late February/early March
a tidewrack of road sand & corrosive salt
gorging street gutters, bunions hardening
on brain cells, & needle-nosed greyhounds, formerly
sprinters at dead-end racetracks, hooded now
in walking blankets of polyester fleece & leashed
to the owners who adopted them, narcissus-pale
women with Medicare woes. All creatures
in heavy clothing look connected & friendly tho
from the warm side of a south-facing window—
bossa nova singers with smiles everywhere,
everywhere gym rats, & the occasional mail slot
of a dark niqab or burqa moving past, a pair of
blue-green eyes behind it watching. You like them
at a distance tho, don't you?—& you love loneliness
even more—loneliness, which has ways of flowing
over barriers, hidden from sight because vast.

BRUSH YOUR FINGERS THROUGH YOUR HAIR,
WHY DON'T YOU

"Brush your fingers
through your hair,
why don't you," her mother
had just told her, & Bud Powell too
advised that
had you a wish to play the piano
scout style, you should keep
your fingernails
clipped, hands
as agile
as cat's ears, swiveling,

but this girl, a very tall
mess-hall of a girl even without her bike helmet
(and with it, a skinny, bitstream
Valkyrie holding
a cup of takeout green tea),
out of her accumulated wisdom,
splurging, she

fairly brimmed with a lifetime's worth
of patience
distilled, not an ounce of annoyance
in her as she ignored
her mother—she
might as well have worn
noise-cancelling headphones in honor
of the serene smile
on her lips—

the zealous whiteness of her teeth
a space where even some barrel-assing
ant could see
something of the
generosity some of us
like to think exists. It
just has to exist.

ARRIVING FROM A DESTINATION

Arriving from a destination
where nothing too
evil is spilled, my father—
        do I know him at all?
as I know my neighbors,
even the chubby stock analyst in maroon
October cardigan, the minister's son
who did not
want a lap dance
but got one anyway.

        And my mother, who is she?—
easy to imagine
her as a one-time saintly grifter, with firm brow
and confident, bee-stung
lips, a girl hopping on bum ankle; easier still
to picture her demure smile
at offers of help from a racetrack mark—
        easy, but not true enough.

All parents raise expectations & dash them,
        dash expectations, raise them ...

        Some unlimited, limiting promise of deeper
connection is made by the initial meeting of sperm & egg—
        not just the kindnesses
of "I'm here for you,
no matter what," but those motives
that commit us
to confusion in company
agreeable or not until the end—

as if, only at the end, will we say
who we were to each other, & why—

What is it my daughter sees me as?—

in the distance
swamp lights glimpsed by those with a yen
for breaking & entering.

SCOOTER

Phil Rizzutto, short stop, the Yankees'
Scooter & play-by-play announcer & The Money Store's
madman of an agreeably trustworthy nature,
but invented for me first in war stories
told by my father—
on a South Pacific island naval air station
maybe it'd be fun to put Scooter
in the game, brass thinks
a sports star visitor to war zone
great theater of operations PR—
but basketball, not
civilization-beating baseball, basketball
my father's game—
"I could take him,
he couldn't get by
me": so sayeth Norman
Rivard, testimony of
a former all-state point guard
1942 season Mass state champs
team captain
Durfee High School Fall River;
his torpedoed destroyer sunk
by a two-man Japanese sub
(a sake brewers' assistant & an Imperial War College ensign?),
a few days earlier their suicide mission
had sent my father
to the base, rescued
just in time for Scooter's morale-boosting
visit, the two together on an asphalt court
in cosmic time, Holy Cow!—

an immortal, lucky accident—
but will, pride, intensity
count more for Norman—"don't depend on luck
OK, why don't you just apply yourself?"
my father's question, frustrated by
his distracted, blurry
son—
apply yourself, stay on track,
stick to it, that's the thing,
you'll adhere
successfully to whatever you want
(not sure I know what the wanting is for even now),
you can be
an architect, trial lawyer, oncologist, surveyor,
if only you apply yourself—
like a wing decal on the model
of a Mustang P-51 Fighter
or whisky dried in a glass-sized ring
on a liquor cart?—
skim the ear wax off your ear drums,
Dad—here is your poet, & here
is your poem.

WHAT'S IT TO YOU?

"What's it to you, Moby Dick?"—now
that's a line I like—so long as the question
signals a syndicate of dark forces to set
myself against—but pursuit of an answer
brings what exactly?—freedom?—dignity?—
it happens, but only rarely. Contemptuous
of management & business school students
from Sloan or Harvard drinking kamikaze
shots of Cuervo Gold or grappa at the bar,
I hate their money-hot talk & greed,
those I imagine as the disguised motherfuckers
of mood swing & avarice & just as willing
on the way to a pig roast or christening to rob
the postman twice if it means they might
feel their vertebrae aligned with the planets.
Zbigniew Herbert says the central problem
is that there are always too few souls for
humanity. Don't know about that. Not one
nanosecond of peace tho will come to pass
through hate being hard on the world . . .
even the hopeless captain in dumb pursuit
of the dumb helpless whale must have
felt that once or twice. Get rid of all
that toxicity by sweating it out, says Rivard—
this ocean called the Atlantic might
be a good place to start—try to swim
now to some courteous and/or forgiven land
that isn't under a spell. If there is one.

WORKRULES

Split the forked tongue further
and you'll find a perfectionist happy
to tell you that you'll just have to love him
as is
if you want him to be kind,
tho the milkers of vipers for venom know better
than to trust
such a grievous & nasty shareholder.
Turf wars & scrums   & more turf wars—
it's a losing bet, with or without a tutor.
The legislators & policymakers are equipped
with insolent voices
and a zest for full-frontal nudity.
They latch on to the affirmative
like a toothache to a priest,
and we suffer their influence.
Some of us stand startled in doorways
as weasels in packs flood
from the wildwood
with a suburban confidence.
Some of us kryptonite our bikes to February street signs
and understand there is more
to the faraway summer than anyone can possibly see.
And in the barrio nuevo
and on post office steps & at the Yale Club & the puppy mill
there is an abundance of eyes
staring, head down, into a facecloth-sized screen
full of liquid crystals.
The echoes of field hollers
and chain-gang chants are there

for anyone to hear who has an ear
for the new workrules.
We all have these me's that wish to be set free at dawn,
amid such pagans as we have become with every heartbeat.
But the outcome of this epic
vendetta might be a rash that you can only pick up
from the neurotoxins of dead people—
our neighbor's daughter
says she caught it from a guy she danced with
at a Paris disco,
a horseboy with hypoglycemic charm—
he must have been a serial killer.

BLOOD LIKE MILK

Blood like milk gone bad—in the hothouse of talk
that passed for thinking in the 70s a radical praxis—
every act of destruction & sabotage a politics
of class solidarity—even murder an imaginable act,
a public revenge on the machinery of state—just talk—
except when it wasn't—Aldo Moro kidnapped & shot
by the *Brigate Rosse,* his body dumped in the trunk
of a red Renault 4 on Via Michelangelo Caetani—talk—
a gabfest of serpents in whose conspiracies the world
soured in clots & was left to rot in a galvanized pail—
the forest overgrew it but the pail still stinks & no one
can find it or wants to. Guilts, shame & amazement
at having believed even briefly that killing might
be justified—on the way to a perfected world—is that
what I wanted?—thirty years later I'm one of many
household names suspicious as always of the banks
and military contractors but placated & footloose
while walking in dreams where I've built hurricane walls
against the blurred, blue cherrywood rain that falls
each day onto our inalienable rights—forced to sing
King Alpha's song in a strange land, you say?—
as my acceptance cannot be defined differently
from despair, & since tightrope walkers & housewives
alike are handcuffed by the busload to briefcases
heavy with debt restructurings, I can only hope
for some change to take place—some basic alteration
in the gene code—my descendants having finally
put behind them these dwarf woods, come at long last
to the age of artificial meat & regenerative healing.

KID CHARLEMAGNE

On the paper's front page the crimes of gang leaders
spoken of as newsworthy in Beacon Hill locker rooms
and Dot Ave workshops, but back of the Metro section
half-forgotten Owsley Stanley, 76—"the artisan of acid"—
dead in Queensland, Australia, crashed—jewelry-making
picked up in prison & eclipse-proof audio engineering
the twin skills of his life beyond the brewing of LSD—
his children—pining, devastated—have planted
an oar in the sandy embankment where a week ago,
inexplicably, he'd ditched his car into a tree, the piper
paid at last for having picked the celestial locks.
Some of us get to burn on the obituary pages
like moonlight on the Ganges burning the bodies already
burnt to ashes by untroubled fire in earlier sunlight—
each man's story is the story of a rake's progress,
each woman's song is chickenskin music & curses
raging against the rake who cowers inside a commuter.
Each story is the story of someone in a comic strip—
his speech balloon overinflated he floats above
those who think they knew him, listening:
"His was the acid behind the Acid Tests," "He
believed that a coming Ice Age would annihilate
the Northern Hemisphere," "In a song he hated,
the singer called him Kid Charlemagne,"
"A heart attack he suffered in the 90s he ascribed
to eating broccoli as a child, forced on him
by his mother"—avatar of the melting horizon
he leaves behind an ocean where an empty rowboat
drifts slowly on the indecipherable water.

SALARYMAN

In the plume of smoke rising
from a volcano on the coast of Iceland,
papery sheets of ash—each ripped square
like a note safety-pinned
to a child's woolen coat
but torn off by a roadside wind—

a missing explanation—

"Please help this boy," the note reads,
"he is a good boy. Give him only
what is needed. He will be
neither genius nor dolt. He likes thinking
(as if thinking were the same
as swimming). When he hears
the hum of bees in the honey locust
teach him that a barge song
is what the bees sing. Remind him
that the lake is there for him to swim—
he doesn't always need to think. This
is a world where a shy salaryman
with a handful of supermarket roses
wrapped in cellophane has to walk
under a sky full of falling rain—
tell this boy the threadbare & blushing
could use a spokesman too."

I CAN'T SPEAK SO

I can't speak so easily of why all's noise
that bothers me of late because can't
hear myself think that well amid the sawing
and hammering of non-union carpenters,
never mind the drunk singing of backyard
neighbors, who after all just want to
live a little & not interrogate themselves
as to the soul & its arrangements (which are
mostly secret—the soul coming & going
like a message banded to a pigeon's leg,
and just as light), but perhaps my mother's
quietness got to me as a child & so
I now crave more of same I associate
with her either loving or anxious
in preoccupied pacing in the sun parlor
or park playground her feelings & thoughts
as they crossed the airspace a tone
unspoken but there to catch, a spell, her signal
subtle but clear—the brain is an antenna
for the mind, the French say (or so Sarah
Stickney tells me), & maybe by being so
can pick up on what's inaudible to ears
but clear even amid the shouting that
surrounded one once as a child sliding gleefully
on fresh sawdust the apprentice butchers
had scattered over varnished oak planking
in the President Avenue meat market—my
mother's look that day somewhere in silence
a question I still can't answer—"why are you
doing that?"—*why?*—*I dunno*—why do I

even need to know?—not a single answer
in my head really—just a vibration—the vexed
but coppery-bright buzz that likewise
comes if you cup a loud cricket in your hand.

STANDOFF

I like reality. I like Rome
                especially, its diesel fuel
and roasted coffee beans
                intact & on the feast day
of San Lorenzo di Perugia or
                thereabouts a plate of spinach & sliced
sausage to eat (the whole
                concoction dished up on *torta al testo,*
a sort of primeval bread);
                I like to see a manhole
struck by a snowplow too—
                maybe because it's an accident,
and some of what happens
                by accident occasionally
(or more than occasionally)
                ought to be thought
a gift?—the sparks
                kicked out by the plow blade
blowing like thin solar flares
                across a dark, snowy street;
and the *princessas*—it's good
                to have them singing on the radio
while I drive across town—all
                of those merrymaking, anorectic
young women close at hand then,
                those newsworthy extroverts
with their dependencies & shitty screen tests
                and tabloid donkey-punches to spare;
ditto the peonies I planted
                with Michaela, circa 1992—

I love their heatstruck scent—
          it almost always surprises me—
I can't quite explain it,
          it's as if I've forgotten the smell
existed—that resinous spill
          (like the fragrance of sandpapered
sandalwood) an oxygen
          that gets sucked into my lungs
then circulated & recirculated
          via the usual bloodways
before being returned
          unconsciously to air.
I like all of these things
          coming & going in time;
recognize too the sheer actuality
          of ongoing, normalized, transnational
violence, the cruelty provoked
          by finance & ideology, the digital
ghettos & branding tactics that
          permit us to hide (& be hidden from)
factory farms, race prisons, toxic debt
          pools, fished-out seas, & sex slaves—
the security of the state being based
          on the anxiety of the citizen,
and evil being said to walk
          the world around us, I see that our self-
betrayals build collateralized
          drones & weaponized viruses,
and that god hunger leads to hate
          and hate to suicide bombings

and threat-assessment maps. Life
                    is everywhere, & to that extent
obvious, dazzling, stunned,
                    stunted, treacherous, & dear;—
things that exist exist, & everything
                    is or is not on their side;—
but I still live more than
                    half my life in my head,
distracted by whatever crops up
                    in there. As adamant as a jayhawk,
I often feel as though I've entered
                    a standoff between what
happens around me & what's
                    going on inside—& this life
that goes on & on inside my head
                    goes on & on & on it seems
almost without me, as
                    it has since childhood,
and I continue to be caught up
                    in all of its head trips,
on the lookout for something
                    I can't put a name to,
never mind find. The clocked day
                    is starting up again,
the morning more than
                    open-ended if you're
me & brained with vague
                    espresso stirrings. Think
of a room whose door
                    stands ajar in a dream—

in the attic of a house where
            you've lived for over fifty years,
a room that you've never
            entered, never even known
existed, but that you walk into
            now: there's a bridge—steel-
girdered, rusty—arcing
            high above an ocean you can see
from that room's window
            (tho it may not be a window
that you're staring out of but a hole
            someone hacked into the roof
with an axe, an opening made by a man
            who must've felt he'd be forgiven).
What I've been looking for
            in my head is like *that*—exactly
as baffling, vast, elemental,
            hopeful, & threatening
as that—but different.

(Civitella Ranieri 2012/Cambridge 2015)

FLICKERING

"I see you," she says—
one of the flickering homeless, with gray
alehouse hair, pale blue

eyes, crunchy lips—a methadone-
troubled moth by the YMCA—but who
does she see?—is it

the chubby, right-handed schoolboy
sent out by the nuns
at St. Joseph's to clap

the chalkboard erasers clean?
Or the giddy
teenage shipping clerk at lunch break

smoking pot for the first time
behind a curtain factory
shed? Perhaps the middle-aged

mortgagee? Maybe an ex-
proofreader in lawyerland or betraying husband?
Maybe the good loser? How about

the new father smiling in tears?
Why not
the complainer's

ally, or the devoted wanker,
or the inert
doubter, or the annoyancer

or toddler?—
if not the circumspect bald man,
crank, or

unselfish lecturer.
Or does she see each of them?—
maybe each

would like
a lantern to carry;
tho there are

nowhere
near enough lamps
for all.

CHOSEN

Made for nudity
not opulence
the sunlight here sways a bit—

a day when you feel almost sure
you've been chosen for something fateful—

or is it just the fennel bush
that trembles?—
like a galaxy quivering at its weightless tips.

Either way,
as the locals say:
you were born to be a blind man's dog—
one of those
the farmers sometimes breed
to keep a watch
for lightning—the kind
who stands for hours
in a stony field, daring dark clouds
to split an oak.

BOOKISH

The bookishness that is
a fever for those
who catch it at all times
lay upon me like a glamour
as far back as middle school,
even if none of my 9th grade friends—
those future bagmen
each on the lookout for a girlfriend ready
to leap like a reawakened Briseis—
even if none believed in words
quite as much as I did.
They were just boys
and not particularly meaner or more lethal
than others, not piggish
or out to spit on the snowdrops & violets
every time some tachycardic flower
sprang up before them.
They just liked to spit.
A massive carelessness governed their world.
They belonged to the good gangs
in partisan gullies
and seemed to have it
all figured out,
while I stood startled in the department store
where husky boys shopped,
a wearer of clip-on Windsor knots
and black-framed eye glasses.
I was a walker on the outskirts
of the visible world
who lived in books

where mossbacked Romans plotted
revenge, pages
in which a clammer's lantern shimmered
above a sleeping geisha's face
or a man stood before a firing squad
remembering how his father
had told him it was the gypsies who invented ice—
every day had the slow, stealthy feel
of a small cargo ship
carrying a stowaway to another home.
Sometimes when the house I live in
is ballsy with sunlight my readiness for life can seem
either very large or very small now.

THAT YEAR

I meet Margaret Mead that year—
"that old lady,
what a pain in the ass she is!"—
so her helper says,
a dreadlocked Dominican from Yonkers;
but outside her suite
at the Museum of Natural History
in the corner turret high above 77th & Columbus
after she's pottered off
I take photos of the shadow puppets
she'd collected in Bali
alongside Bateson, her ex-husband Gregory
Bateson—he'd divorced her & moved on
to cybernetics & the study of
dolphin speech, the mammal chatter
he'd reported
hearing in Caribbean waters
as feedback, coded & algorithmic—
life was a construction of encoded systems,
my teachers claimed—
the epic stories these puppets played out
in the *wayang kulit,* each propped for an eternity
or two against a white sheet,
the bejeweled warriors & courtesans
killer gods & goddesses
Ganesh, the Remover of Obstacles
Rama, Sita, Hanuman, Arjuna,
the projected lives of all
the monkey lords & cloud dwellers—
my life near Exit 8 off the Jersey Pike

next door to Jim & Cyndi,
friendly potheads & printer's devils—
1976—my shantytown year in New Jersey
at the graduate school of anthropology—
a rake's progress already in progress there
each week
as I deal pot & acid to moneyed undergrads
in the eating clubs at Princeton
all the while
reading Lacan & Levi-Strauss,
a kinship economy of the sort
referred to in passing by Clifford Geertz
when he lectures in March
at the Institute for Advanced Study—
he quoted Olson then:
"The first fact of America is space,"
a fact so obvious
its implications were made impossible
to prove either true or false—
my teachers were wrong—
there is no code,
no use for the beautiful
and ornate key they pressed so
eagerly into my hands.

LATE JANUARY PROTEST AGAINST THE BETRAYERS

In his leather snap cap & undertaker's suit of
shiny polyester black, one of those resisters
of the transmitted order—an aging Marxist lost boy—
alarm all over his shyly determined, axe-sharp face,
tho a shadow falls upon that face, a gloom
cast by the screen flash of corporations gaming
the go-flo of dollars & broadband—he stands
with umbrella outside Starbucks & silently
hands out pamphlets, shucked by cold tourists.
Does he have set rounds at subway stations
and parks full of volatile sleepwalkers? Maybe
he haunts the doorway of Filene's at tag end
of Presidents' Day sales? Does he have a day job?
Wife or boyfriend? For change of pace does he
sit with coffee in his tiny kitchen scanning
the box scores of road-trip double-headers?
Or is he always thinking how the world should
be righteous, justice at hand?—like my old
teacher in the dim Boston University lecture hall,
Howard Zinn—*your life,* he said, *drives*
history—you can't be neutral on a moving train—
he died yesterday at 87 but left with his view
still alive & intact of liberation possible for all.

COMMON

The American common is no collective or princedom
but privacies of need & pleasure as they intersect
in public spaces, tho the insufferable powers that be
breed their plots behind our backs, thinking us
witless, seemingly blind to their afflicted intentions,
just a bunch of demographic motormouths & screw-ups
to be targeted by commodities traders & search engines—
a marketing niche for every need, stereotypes
tagged by algorithms—*here* is a typical team
of baton twirlers in an airport bar, each of them clad
in foxy red track suits & tuned-in to the dollhouse
stimulations of pigeon-talking sales reps; *there*
is a previously undetected aggregation of retirees,
evangelical camp kids, kickass bowlers,
and mothy nuns in starched wimples, for whom
the news of the day means the aging boy-man
Hugh Grant's fear of double chins—neither of
these or any other data dump entirely false,
but so narrow-minded sometimes as to lose sight
of us entirely: the midtown lady in Capris,
a four-square surgeon off-duty & headed out
to play poker, the plumber fly-fishing by the river—
a sky of twilight slate now—not a word written on it.

NEWS CYCLE

The news feed careening from horrible
to funny in an eye-blink,
erasing itself
neatly—like this seemingly
cheery bulletin from war valley Waziristan,
reporting drones killed them all
(what's cheerful about that?
who's *them* so unlike us?), the dead
supposed jihadi
chased away then
by a story on generational change
in genital fashions—
hairy pussy poised to make a comeback?—
the backlot buzz
around director Ang Lee & his Woodstock comedy,
when many would-be extras
for hippie crowd scenes
arrived at the shoot with shaved pubes, unfit
to play their parents & grandparents
naked as it happened
in mud-sodden thunderstorms
August '68—the news
careening from funny to horrible,
erasing memory
itself . . .

SECOND CHANCES

What's left?
Is it a wisdom
worthy of amateur status?—
to be loved in particular for all
its perplexing infrequency.
There is a gate
inside nearly every intuition
it's true
and many of these gates have opened
of late to a future
at the occupier's compound,
a zone where
right around the time the ambassador's sigh
comes to a stop
like a broken arrow among sequoias
a quick sponge bath
might be in order.
But within another gate
the giant anointed with sandalwood instructs
those who go to sleep aggrieved
by angry conversations
and shifting loyalties
to wake up,
so that the redness of the poppies
can be seen in a brazen light—
he advises all of us
to shun the iron wheel for which
a warlord's lips
kissed the earth. On the issue
of second chances

two things are now totally clear:
at some point soon I will watch
a run of rain squalls
rippling across the groggy Atlantic;
meanwhile, our cat will
continue to smack at the window screen
with blinded paws,
the damp flutter of
white wings on that moth it hunts
having already escaped north.

LUCKY DAY STILL

Lucky day still spent wrestling the private problems
and obsessions encountered first in your youth
but played out now within the spectacle of public aging
(tho, strangely, as you age you feel less & less seen
by the young, a citizen active in frequencies of light waves
increasingly invisible—not even *boring* to 15-year-olds).
Of course, some problems you once had really have
vanished—you can sense that as your daughter lays out
the tactics crucial to "pre-gaming," her teen friends
setting out to get toasted or stoned before house parties,
parties at which they've been warned not to drug or drink—
no longer a worry for you (except as relates, of course,
to your daughter)—you can drink & drug somewhat
"it would seem" to your heart's content. Not your style,
you say? Not any longer? Still, the urge to lift or get
lifted from self-conscious woes hasn't gone away totally,
has it? Wanting to be free of your self has always
been a mission big in your church—evangelically so!
You got in a way (the wrong way) your wish—
your skin certainly got looser on you—baggy, rounder,
wrinkled—prescriptions for departure—the rigging's
untuned, & no milk bath full of rose hips can compensate
(so your friend likes to say), no fish oil omega-3
in gel capsules manufactured by entrepreneurial ex-hippies
no wifely fruit smoothies or mod boots will cure
jowls now or allow for glamour without the costume.

ESCAPISM

Two older ladies with gray hair tinted
red, cranberry-red, hip pointers have them
waddling on *Cinco de Mayo*—it's here
in public places that the elders arrive at slow times
and boredoms they may not have feared so
as prepared for by practicing with years
of dull routines—*my* favorite morning pastime
toast & coffee with my head sunk far below
the fold, miles deep into newsprint & diving down
through stories reported by journalists half-blind
and jacked-up on global catastrophes gone to seed.
Apricot jam dripped onto your chauffeur-black
pajama leg is a pleasure to lift with an index finger
and lick, even if not quickly enough to keep it
from dripping again—this time onto your sleeve
and the Papal Nuncio's nose—the anxieties of
news escaped—sort of. "Escaped the nets,
escaped the ropes—moon on water," so states
the spring moon's job description, according
to Buson, the scourge of chrysanthemum growers,
whom he thought of as slaves to flowers—
but isn't it that some things are better to be
slaves to than others?—so I woke early
this morning, my poor head sick of duties
assumed at the remote behest of one bureaucracy
or another, & thought then of you naked
in a bathtub one pentecostal August
30 years ago, & your dark nipples somewhere
in memory near the sudsy waterline

put an end to the busywork of headquarters,
they destroyed paperwork & telephone calls
to come—it was so nice to meet you there,
and to go on soaking with you in my head.

THIS

I rode the highball, I fired the daylight—
I warmed my hands on
the back of your thighs, a tan inch
below your panties,
wanting to die like Jesus
but without the windshear & miracles
save the one
for being reborn over
and over again for as many of those
minutes in which I would kneel before you
on this Dutch siesta—

> what was it Sappho said of your dress
> pooled there on the floor 3,000 years ago?—
> "better that transparent muslin from Kos
> than a hoplite army of warriors"—

this pleasure as
people have it sometimes
wintering-over
and naked as it comes & goes,
this was hours before our dinner of *osso buco*.
That I am a professional prizefighter
is a fact as well known as that
I am a man who has feared no one
in this life, either inside the ring
or out—I can't say I like
to write love letters—hardly at all—
but this
which I write to you now is true.

WHAT SHE SAID

"It's not," she said, "that I want
to be invisible, just that
sometimes I turn sideways a little
so less of me can be seen,
like I don't want the attention,
or I feel trapped, or something"—
in her father's room, the tone arm
on the turntable descending slowly,
the needle like a black wasp's,
the wasp filling his assisted-living
bedroom with its knock shop
song, & the nurse's aide futzing
with freshly laundered sheets
as the stung chords of the guitar
break beneath a hillbilly twang,
his room revolving then
for years like some jook
joint full of sea changes—
"maybe you think it's just
that I'm in a hurry to leave,"
she said, "like I'm looking
to get saddled-up again"—
but I knew she remembered
the fox (if it really was a fox)
dying by the waterfall, & the blood
matted on its fur, & I had that
redness in my mind too, redder
blood on reddish fur, its dark wet-
ness a thing to leave behind—
as if such a thing could be left.

CALL & RESPONSE

In this last
book by Zbigniew
Herbert, *Elegy*

for the Departure,
in a poem
titled "Chord"

a previous reader
has underlined the passage
that ends

the poem—
"truly truly I tell you
great is the abyss

between us
and the light"—
and written

alongside
it 4 words—
"our my

anguish
melancholia"—protest?
consoling note

of empathy? or cry
for help
against the cyclonic

injustice
of an unhappy
life?—

on one side
of the page 14
words by

the poet dead now
10 years;
on the other, 4 words

printed neatly
by a living man or woman,
troubled, nameless.

TAKE IT ON THE HEEL

What's it all for?
Sins & good deeds
end up equal in eternity—
each of them like a sunflower seed
reflected in a raven's eye
in the moment before it's eaten.

TO ROTATE

Not that you didn't
care, but that you couldn't see
that you did, couldn't
even feel it
in your fingers at first, clamped as you were
by everything
that had made you angry—
that was the problem.
It was a fine day to be loosened by stains tho,
even if miserable about the ticket & tow.
It was a fine day to buzz.
To rotate through a patois.
To unfold in the flux
of a despicable mobile home
made to do double-wide
duty as an office.
At the tow company car lot
the office heater did what
it could—it floated the sour sauce
from the half-eaten bowl
of canned spaghetti & mixed it
with the fug that hung about
an elderly German shepherd,
his balls dangling between
spindly legs like black pudding stones
set permanently asway—
the dog's left hind leg nicked
by a tow truck
on some ancient, forgettable day—
his pelvic zone

off-kilter, the leg kinked by a limp.
"I didn't hit him, he
walked in front of me," snorts
the billing clerk
and Chancellor of the Exchequer,
a fathead.
And to stroke such a dog's face
at such a moment
is to indemnify the kindness in you,
no matter how small—
your tenderness reveals itself
as the wheelchair ideogram stenciled onto asphalt
to save the parking space
reveals itself
when ice melts—slowly.

TOMAS

Tranströmer to me, after
I'd told him
of the place I'd lived three months on Lidingö,
suburban Stockholm island, former servant's quarters
(a maid for the big house with its gingerbread shingles?),
the yard aspens & maples, birches
by the quiet cove,
and left on the lawn
an old clawfoot tub
that the owners
claimed Greta Garbo had bathed
in—
"there must be
many bathtubs people are saying
that about
on Lidingö"—so
he told me—& I believed him.
One of the taller enigmas, with a kingfisher's smile.
Amused.
The one man with
a valid theology.

EXCELLENCE

It's true that
Luca Signorelli gave even
Michelangelo

ideas, but
exiting from the duomo
in Orvieto

the excellence
of sunlight still seems
greater to me

than Signorelli.
How great? As great as a cicada
in dry sawgrass

awakened
like a spark; or so it might
feel to you too

if you'd grown up
next door to a casket maker's
storehouse—a Quonset

hut, salvaged
War Department junk—its galvanized
corrugated sheet metal

like chrome rubbed raw & dull
by steel wool
and shivering hot at noon—

that metal would burn you,
burn you good & sorry
if you touched your

fingers to it
while peering through
the grimy windows,

all those market-rate
coffins stacked inside on sawhorses
and dark as lead doorways.

OLIVE TREES

Steaming on this sunny hill,
like fat sultanas huddled
on the benches of a sweat lodge,

these olive trees have
a way of letting you know
you've been taken off
the waitlist & accepted—

it's tempting,

    their advice:

        try to relax;

don't be kissless in the summer dark—

don't be the darkling pawn in summer,
don't do it by the book;
be the chinois orange of the poppies;

if hope is crushed, try forgiveness.

MICHAEL MAZUR

Did you really
have to show up on the Doppler
like scroll master Guo Xi
of the Northern Song
dynasty?—
short answer: yes:
clouds & light
at rest on tide water:
the marine layer
in your paintings
a cousin to calm mist upcountry
and sister to the seething heaven falling
all at once over the lankiest salt hay
and most barbarian
sand dunes east of the Yangtze estuary.
Who am I speaking to anyhow?
Mike. He's here, on this screen
in these words,
the friend no longer hurtling
forward in any
noticeable way. No he's not,
he isn't here. Don't say so—
even if the night
ends as it does
once a month with the morning
warning no parking on the odd-numbered
side of the street—"you will
be tagged & towed"—
even if all
blood hurries to love

other blood
loving the sun
that shines after street cleaning
by the cab stand
as Rosh Hashanah picks up
speed, everywhere
at once.

FREEDOM IN THE MIDST

Freedom in the midst of necessity means us
to be less willful than watchful & alert
if following without complaisance the divining rod
of what is given—still, the fallacy of the self
insists that a change is gonna come, change
that lasts, & at home again forever then
this time we will be happy—happy, calm, flawless,
and complete—a mistake, but totally forgivable,
as most days blundering's the whole human
story—like the terrible fact that you died
in a soft rain, having fallen (accidentally or not)
from the top of those tall soccer field bleachers.
I knew you 20 years, & didn't, ever.
I liked you, then didn't . . . or else did & didn't.
Now friends write me emails of felt regrets
pressing their dismayed & curious ears closer
to your death. *What happened?* they ask—
a question without an answer—our confusion
confusing itself further—an error that time
will no more reveal the purpose of
than clarify the wishes of your beautiful face—
as they say in the ballads, a curl-framed face.

GHOSTS ON THE ROAD

A bookkeeping man,
tho one sure to knock on wood,
and mostly light at

loose ends—my friend
who is superstitiously funny, & always
sarcastic—save once,

after I'd told him
about Simone's first time
walking—a toddler,

almost alone, she'd
gripped her sweater, right hand
clutched

chest-high, reassured
then, she held on to herself
so, so took a few

quick steps—
oh, he said, you know what? Leonard
Cohen, when he was 13,

after his father's
out-of-the-blue heart attack, he slit
one of the old man's

ties, & slipped a
message into it, then buried it
in his backyard—

he's 73 now, & can't
recall what he wrote—threadbare
heartfelt prayer perhaps,

or complaint—
his first writing anyway.
The need to comfort

ourselves is always
strongest at the start,
they say—

do you think
that's true? my friend asked.
I don't, he said,

I think the need
gets stronger, he said, it
just gets stronger.

DARKHORSE

The bright barge of sunlight
carries you as it drifts
across the oakwood floor—

that's the charm of traveling
while staying put,
sitting there in your chair
while the sun voyages slowly along;
a journey for one man alone.

Then it has to be noon,
because the gangplank has dropped,
the direct sun
having vanished—
my game plan changed—

an arrival has taken place.

It gets like that
with memory,
sometimes some small, previously unheeded
piece of the past
will wait for you
to disembark—

it doesn't come to you,
you reach it

at a certain
age. My age now
the same more or less as my father's
the day he took me
to see the curator of milk teeth,

when we stopped to sit awhile
among the call girls brunching in the bar
at the Hotel New Yorker,
their sunglasses staring down at scrambled eggs
and lox on bagels—

I heard one of them
say the word—*darkhorse.*

Darkhorse.

—Don't forget: I asked for
two white horses to do the pulling
at my burying ground:

the way-forsaking beauty & the king of ways.

THE MOON IN TIME LAPSE

The moon in time lapse sliding over skyline
the way a remote frisbee might wheel through air
as slowly as a banjo once floated across the wide
Missouri River in my mind when as a boy
the devil to pay permitted me to dream-up
my getaway from home, far from my parents'
witchy vigilance & the wine-barrel cellars
of their household—this after my experimental
stuffing of a dinner fork into a light socket
in the green gazebo under backyard grapevines.
That fuse box blown & blackened was the bliss
of departure—it was thrilling, but sometimes
I have to stop to touch my life & see if it's real.
How surprising to find that I wanted so much,
and mostly got it. My fantasies are fewer now
(one involves living through a day without
resentments, the other getting seated next to
gorgeous Fanny Ardant on a puddle jumper).
No need to see my life as a story the world
has got to read, no need for sentimental
mooning & nostalgia—blessed with a bit
of amnesia anyway, I don't recall much
of what went down. I know that it's engraved
there on some cellular level, & that I can't
command the consequences—like a spider
perched atop a survey stake in a bull-
dozed field, I feel slightly truer in any case.

HERE WE GO

The rag that swiped the skate blades clean
    of slush, drying now

        in the trash barrel, a 50-gallon fire
           burning up the teahouse trash

and samurai armor, those dragon scales
    humbler than the pants that boys put on
    between 5th grade & 6th

        behind a levee, rain on the river

"rain; empty river; a voyage"

like carrier pigeons flying home, footsteps
    on a run of wooden stairs

        near the wildwood,
           where a swallow dies of hunger,
           winter's end

in costume, & all by itself,
    the sunset

        a red bowling shirt with black piping
           on the collar

going forth with vehemence
    into darkness, the rebbe's daughter, hot as ever

for Benya Krik, the wish to be something forbidden
　　　or flavorful as always

　　　　　on the skinny legs of the pert, a taste

　　　　brined in boatyard puddles, the reflections of a yacht
　　　　　that drips seawater in November

when hoisted up, glorious & miserable,
　　　a wall calendar that had fallen

long ago, the child having been born
　　　at last, sloppy & lawless,
　　　the 2nd day of December, 1953—

　　　　　Here we go, I thought, face down
　　　　　in autumn's indispensable blue pillow book,
　　　　　here we go again, full speed ahead.

ACKNOWLEDGMENTS

Thanks to the editors of those locations in which these poems appeared in earlier versions:

The American Poetry Review, Congeries, The Cortland Review, Forklift, Ohio, The Green Mountains Review, Gulf Coast, Memorious, New Ohio Review, Pangyrus, Ploughshares, Plume, Provincetown Arts, Tin House, and *Tuesday; an Art Project.*

"News Cycle," "Common," and "Escapism" were published first in the anthology *Devouring the Green: Fear of a Human Planet* (Jaded Ibis Press).

"The Moon in Time Lapse" was featured at poets.org (the Academy of American Poets website) as part of its "Poem Flow" project, and printed as a limited-edition broadside by the University of Arizona Poetry Center/ Book Arts Collaborative in Tucson.

"Ghosts on the Road" appeared on the Poem-a-Day program at poets.org, and "Lucky Day Still" on Poetry Daily at poems.com.

My thanks as well to the Civitella Ranieri Foundation for the gift of time and good company at their center for the arts in Umbria, where some of these poems were begun.

David Blair, Maria Chelko, Michael Collier, Stuart Dischell, Jennifer Flescher, Mark Gosztyla, David Guenette, Katie Peterson, and Sarah Stickney all offered encouragement and advice as the manuscript for this book evolved. Fred Marchant, Jeff Shotts, Tom Sleigh, and Michaela Sullivan saved the author from several serious errors of judgment. Nothing but gratitude from me to them.

DAVID RIVARD is the author of five other books of poetry: *Otherwise Elsewhere, Sugartown, Bewitched Playground, Wise Poison,* winner of the James Laughlin Award of the Academy of American Poets and a finalist for the *Los Angeles Times* Book Prize, and *Torque,* winner of the Agnes Lynch Starrett Prize. His poems and essays appear regularly in the *American Poetry Review, Ploughshares, Poetry, Poetry London, Tin House,* and other publications. Among his awards are fellowships from the Guggenheim Foundation, the Civitella Ranieri Foundation, the National Endowment for the Arts, and the Fine Arts Work Center in Provincetown, as well as the Shestack Prize from the *American Poetry Review* and the O. B. Hardison Jr. Poetry Prize from the Folger Shakespeare Library, in recognition of both his writing and teaching. Rivard currently teaches in the MFA Program in Writing at the University of New Hampshire.

The text of *Standoff* is set in Clifford. Book design by Rachel Holscher.

Composition by Bookmobile Design and Digital Publisher Services, Minneapolis, Minnesota.

Manufactured by Thomson-Shore on acid-free, 30 percent postconsumer wastepaper.